PLAY BALL
with Roger the Dodger

PLAYERS ONLY

PLAY BALL
with Roger the Dodger

by Al Campanis · pictures by Syd Hoff

G.P. Putnam's Sons · New York

To my mother, Mama Tulla, whom I have loved from the day I was born

Library of Congress Cataloging in Publication Data
Campanis, Al.
    Play ball with Roger the Dodger.
    Summary: Outlines ways to improve baseball skills
including batting, catching, baserunning, and sliding.
    1. Baseball—Juvenile literature. [1. Baseball]
I. Hoff, Sydney   II. Title.
GV867.5.C35 1980   796.357'2   80-12483
ISBN 0-399-20710-4
ISBN 0-399-20711-2 pbk.
First Peppercorn paperback edition published in 1980.

Contents

A NOTE FROM TOM LASORDA

Al Campanis has one of the most progressive minds in baseball and he is considered by many to be one of the finest teachers in the game. Al has played a great part in my life, and he taught me more about baseball than any other person I've known. He gave me my first job as a scout and later moved me to a minor league manager's position. Whatever success I've achieved in baseball, I owe a great deal of it to Al Campanis. He has been an inspiration to me and my family throughout the years.

Tom Lasorda

Manager,
Los Angeles Dodgers

Roger is a switch-hitter which means that he can bat either right-handed or left-handed.

CHOOSING A BAT

Pick a bat which feels good to you. A light bat is better than a heavy bat.

Grip the bat with your fingers and with the insides of your hands.

The insides of your hands should be facing each other.

Keep your hand and fingers relaxed and ready for the pitch.

The end grip

The choke grip

HOW TO STAND

Stand in a comfortable position with your legs fairly close together or slightly apart.

Your head and eyes face the pitcher.

Keep your hands and elbows away from your body. This will give you more freedom to swing.

Stand with your body straight up or in a slight crouch.

Keep your shoulders and hips level.

Keep your weight evenly balanced on the balls of your feet.

Hold the bat still. Do not let your hands move down. This is called "hand hitch" and it hurts your timing.

Hold the bat still!

HOW TO SWING

Keep your head and eyes on the ball.

Keep your shoulders level.

Keep your swing level—follow through.

Let your hips turn all the way around.

Take a short, controlled step forward as you swing.

Keep your front leg straight.

Push off from your toes on the back foot.

HOW TO HIT

The Right Way

A straight front leg lets the toes of your back foot use the power of your body.

Your head and the top half of your body should move forward very little.

Getting your hips around quickly will open up your front shoulder.

Your top hand turns over *after* the bat hits the ball.

The Wrong Way

Do not move toward the ball. Let the ball come to you.

You lose power if you step onto your front foot too soon.

If you don't move your hips, you will lose your balance.

You must watch the ball. Your head must not turn. Do not bend your front leg.

OVERSTRIDING

Don't step too far toward the pitcher. This is called "overstriding." Most batters who take a long step toward the pitcher are .200 hitters or poor batters.

**Reach!
Don't step!**

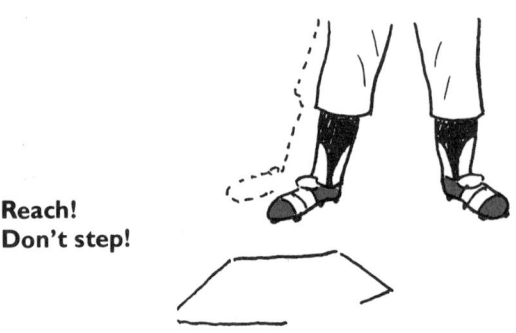

Don't go forward and put too much weight on your front foot. Reach out. Don't take a big step!

THE BATTING TEE

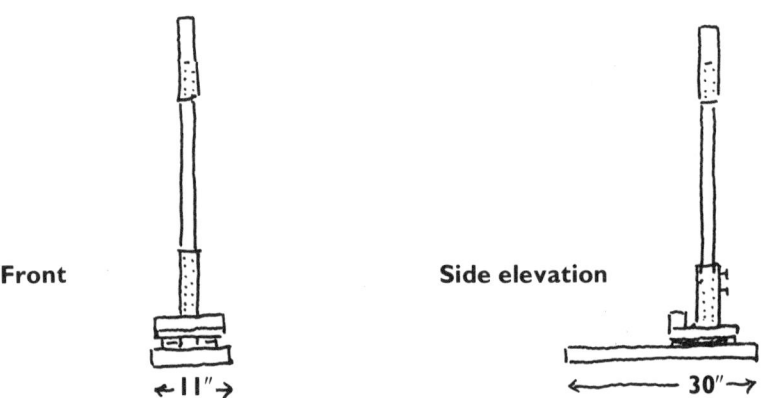

Front

Side elevation

←11"→

←——— 30" —→

Use a batting tee for practice. This is something you can do on your own.

TIPS FOR SWINGING

Watch how my head and eyes are still, following the ball.

Watch how my ear seems to be listening to my shoulder.

Watch how my top hand has turned over my bottom hand *after* I have hit the ball.

My swing is level because my shoulders and hips are level.

My step, or *stride*, is short. I'm *reaching* not stepping.

My front hip turns quickly on this pitch.

THE SHORT FAST SWING

Small half-circle, or *arc*

The bat hits the ball here.

The short swing lets you take a faster swing.

The best time to swing at the ball is when it is over the plate.

The longer you wait to swing, the more time you have to see what kind of pitch is coming at you. You'll swing at fewer "bad" balls.

A fast bat is a sign of long-ball power.

Practice your short fast swing!

THE LONG SLOW SWING

Big half-circle, or *arc*

The bat hits the ball here.

A long swing takes a long time because it is a big arc.

To make a long swing you have to start the swing early. This means that you will swing at a lot of bad pitches.

Most batters who have a slow swing are weak hitters.

Shorten your swing and you will be in the .300 hitter's class!

THE STRIKE ZONE

A pitch is in the strike zone when it is over home plate and between the batter's armpits and his knees.

Know the strike zone.

Learn to hit the ball where it is pitched.

Hold back your swing if the pitch is not in the strike zone.

Good hitters seldom swing at these pitches.

HITTING THE BALL WHERE IT IS PITCHED

Left-hand hitter

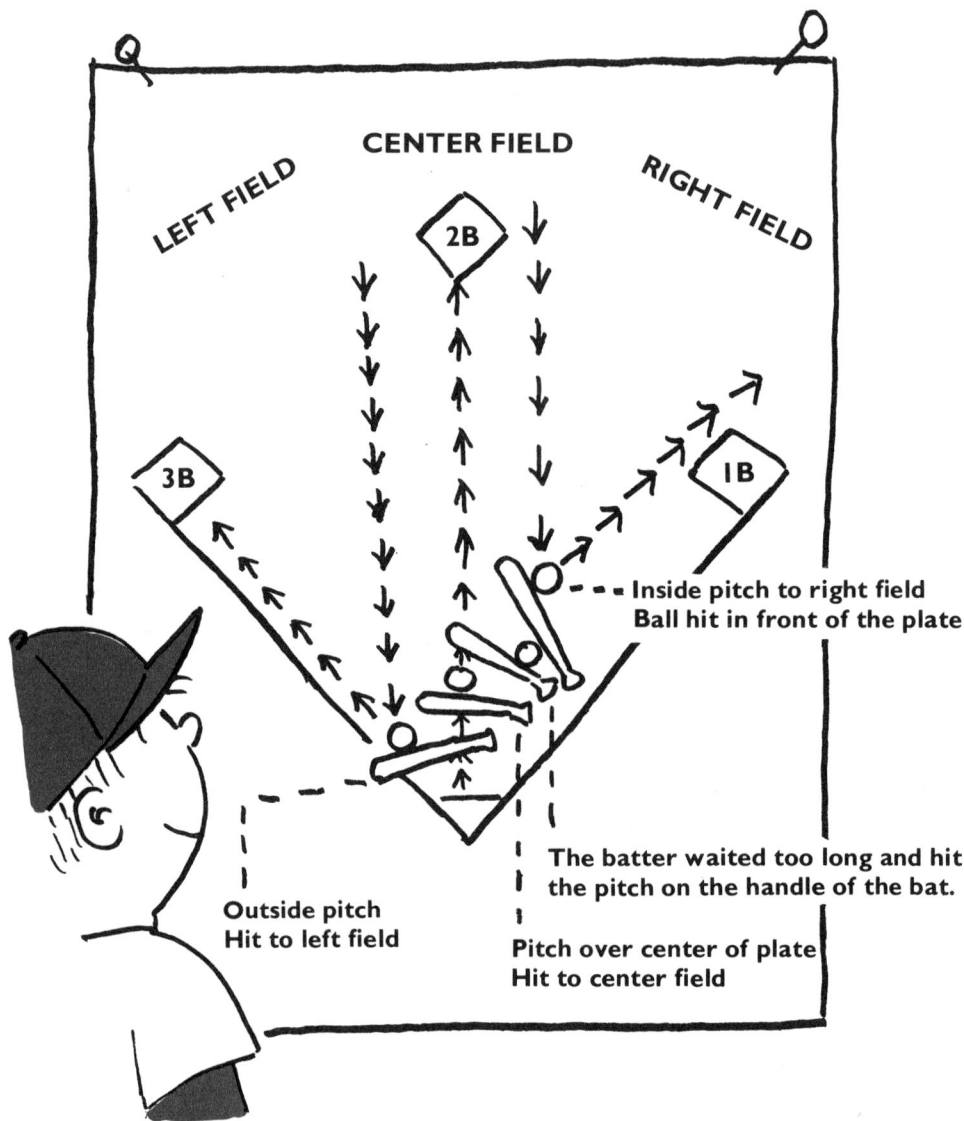

CENTER FIELD

LEFT FIELD

RIGHT FIELD

2B

3B

1B

Inside pitch to right field
Ball hit in front of the plate

The batter waited too long and hit
the pitch on the handle of the bat.

Outside pitch
Hit to left field

Pitch over center of plate
Hit to center field

If you are a right-hand hitter, the position of the bat and where the ball travels shown in the drawing above would be the opposite.

IMPORTANT TIPS

Watch the ball from the time it leaves the pitcher's hand until it hits your bat.

Don't be afraid of being hit by the ball. "Don't step in the bucket!" This is pulling away from home plate.

Stepping in the bucket

Believe in yourself.

Be confident that you can hit any ball from any pitcher.

Be a go-getter at bat! Be a daring hitter!

Bunting is when you hit the ball lightly without taking a swing at it. Bunting is used under certain conditions. A good bunt can make the difference between winning or losing a close game.

There are three types of bunts:

    Sacrifice bunt
    Bunt for a hit
    The squeeze bunt
        The suicide
        The safety

THE SACRIFICE BUNT

Turn your hips just as the pitcher lets go of the ball. Your body and knees are bent slightly with most of your weight on your front foot.

The big part of the bat points toward the pitcher.

Just as the ball meets the bat, there should be a slight give, or pullback of the hands.

Use the bunt when you are up against good pitchers.

Bunt strikes.

THE BUNT FOR A HIT

The Drag Bunt

The drag bunt is used when the first baseman is playing deep, or the pitcher is slow at covering first base.

Make the first baseman field the ball to his right.

The first step when "dragging a bunt" is a crossover step with the back foot.

The big end of the bat faces the pitcher and is in front of your body.

The Push Bunt

The push bunt is used when the third baseman is playing deep, or when the pitcher is slow and a poor fielder.

Don't use the crossover step until the ball is bunted.

The big end of the bat is held behind your body.

Bunt the ball softly and close to the foul line, but in fair ground.

On all bunt plays the top hand guides the bunt.

THE SQUEEZE PLAYS

The suicide, or running squeeze

On the suicide squeeze, you *must* bunt any pitch.

On this play the batter gives the signal to the runner on third base which means: "Yes, I know the suicide squeeze is on!"

As the pitcher's front foot touches the ground, the batter gets ready to bunt. *Not before.*

The runner on third base does not start, or "break," until the pitcher's front foot touches the ground.

On the suicide squeeze the batter should try to bunt the pitch on the ground right back at the pitcher.

The Safety Squeeze

X shows where the runners are.

The safety squeeze is used:

To move the runner on third base home

To sacrifice the runner from first to second base if there are runners on first and third base

On this play the runners do not "break," or leave the base, until the ball is bunted and on the ground.

Baserunning

All baserunning is controlled by how the game is going.

Know the number of outs
   None out
   One out
   Two out

Know the outfielder's arms
   Strong—be careful
   Weak—go—take chances
   Wild—go—take chances

What's the score?

When you are running to first base
   Look at the base. Don't look at the ball.
   Don't slide except to avoid the first baseman's tag.

When you are on first base
   Look at the coach for a signal.
   Check. How many outs are there?
   Where are the outfielders playing?

How to take a lead off first base
   A one-way lead—your weight is mostly on the back foot.
   A two-way lead—your weight is evenly spread on both feet and ready to go two ways—on to second base or back to first base.

The One-Way Lead

Keep most of your weight on the back foot. This lead lets you find out how fast or slowly the pitcher can throw to first base.

Runner's position after pitcher throws home

The Two-Way Lead

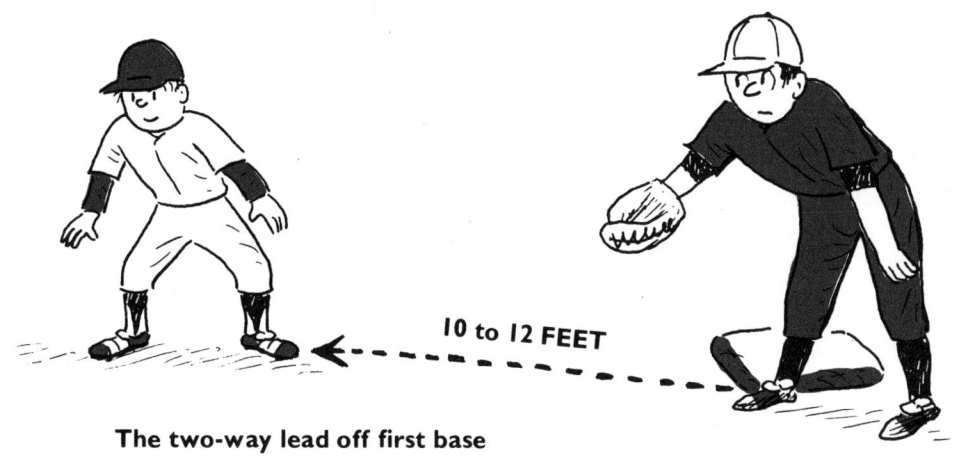

10 to 12 FEET

The two-way lead off first base

The crossover step

This is the lead to take when you want to steal second base. The crossover step is the first and best move to make when stealing.

Put your weight evenly on both feet and you can go two ways—on to second base or back to first base.

HOW TO STEAL

Bases are stolen on pitchers' weaknesses. Here are some of them:

A pitcher who uses a high leg kick gives a runner a good start

A pitcher with his left shoulder too far toward first base

A pitcher who leans toward home plate

High leg kick allows a runner a good start

ROUNDING THE BASES

Look at every base and make sure you touch every base.

Touch the front inside corner of each base.

Dip your shoulder when tagging the base, just the way you do on your bike when you make a left turn.

Be daring and take chances when running bases.

In a slide, you let your body fall to the ground to avoid a tag.

A slide is also used to slow the forward motion of your body.

When in doubt—slide! Your body is ready for a slide and you can get hurt if you stay standing up.

THE FEETFIRST SLIDE

The feetfirst slide

Stay relaxed with your eyes on the base, feet straight out, toes pointed, and hands overhead.

THE BENT LEG SLIDE

The bent leg slide

One leg is bent under the other.

This slide is good for braking speed or if you want to get back up quickly.

THE HOOK SLIDE

The hook slide

The slide begins like the feetfirst slide, but the foot touching the base bends in to a hooked position.

THE HEADFIRST SLIDE

The headfirst slide back to the base

The headfirst slide into a base is dangerous. Do not use it. The only time you go headfirst is going *back* to a base.

OTHER TIMES TO USE A SLIDE

Use a slide to break up a double play. Hit the second baseman's or shortstop's stepping foot with your instep.

When home plate is blocked by the catcher, slide to the side of the catcher and touch the plate with your hand.

THE DEFENSE
In the Field

No pitcher under fourteen should throw curve balls. Throw fast balls overhand.
This will make your arm stronger.

Here is one way to practice an overhand throw.

HOLDING THE BALL

If you throw overhand, hold the ball *across* the seams.

If you are a sidearm pitcher, hold the ball *on* the seams.

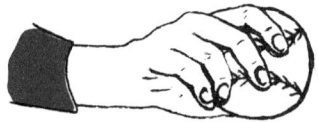

The best way is to hold the ball across the seams and to throw overhand!

HOW TO STAND

Hide the ball behind your hip and then behind your glove.
Your body is bent forward slightly.

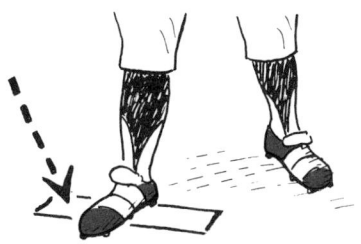

Your front spikes should be in front of the pitching plate.

WHEN THERE IS A RUNNER ON FIRST BASE

Take this position when there is a runner on first base.

The closer the game and the better the runner, the more times you must throw to first base. Keep the runner on his toes!

All pitchers should develop a quick throw to first base and home plate.

Keep a runner close to first base by moving your head quickly toward first base.

THE TURN OR PIVOT TO SECOND BASE

HOME PLATE

2ND BASE

When trying to pick off a runner at second base, turn in the direction of your gloved hand.

Pitcher's turn should be beyond a straight line to second base.

Don't let the runner on second base take a big lead.

Repeat your turn a few times and you will keep runners close to the bag.

THE PITCHER AS A FIELDER

Covering First Base

Move toward first base on all balls hit to your left, line drives, or ground balls.

Run straight for the base, and when you are near it, turn a bit so that you are running inside the foul line.

Getting into Position

Sometimes your body will be in a poor position to field the ball. Get your balance for a good throw by taking a step forward with your stepping foot.

Stand on the front part of your feet when fielding.

Field the ball and *then* look at the base.

On a double play, lead the shortstop. Throw the ball a bit to his left, but right at the second baseman. Throw at face level.

Pitcher-to-shortstop double play

Pitcher-to-second baseman double play

CONTROL

Good pitching probably wins 75% of all games. A pitcher without control will have a hard time winning!

Some of the reasons pitchers don't have control are:

Spikes are on top of the rubber

Not looking at the catcher's glove all the way

Taking too long a step (overstriding)

Throwing across the body instead of straight ahead

Changing the hold on the ball

Not following through

Losing self-control and becoming angry

Spikes in front of rubber
Throwing overhand
Pushing off back leg and driving toward home plate

Good follow-through
Throwing hand is over opposite knee.
Body is bent.
Eyes are looking at catcher's glove.

Pitching off front part of rubber, not on top.
Back knee is bent for driving power.

A good pitcher throws strikes!

Throw the ball over the plate.

Winning pitchers walk very few batters.

Keep your cool.

Don't get mad at yourself and you will be a winning pitcher!

The catcher is very important because you are in the best position to direct the defense and because you are the only one who can see all the players.

GIVING THE SIGNS

Point your right knee at the pitcher.

Keep your right hand deep between your legs.

Put your glove over your left knee.

All of this is done so that the coaches on the other team cannot see your signs.

THE CATCHER'S POSITION

After signaling the pitcher, get into a balanced position. Your feet should be spread apart, knees bent, left foot a bit in front of the right foot.

Your weight should be on the front part of your feet.

Give the pitcher a target to aim for with your glove.

Be as close to the batter as you can without touching the bat.

Keep your hands still.

Your ungloved hand should be in an almost half-closed fist position as you wait to catch the ball.

Catch the ball in the pocket of the glove and immediately cover with the ungloved hand.

Shifting

Shifting to the right   **Shifting to the left**

You should glide or shift to each side. Catchers seldom cross their feet.
Bring pitches just outside the strike zone toward the middle of your body.
When you are receiving a close high strike, bend your knees.
On close low strikes, straighten them.
Practice blocking pitches on the ground.

The Throwing Position

Good throwing depends on balance.

Keep your weight on the back foot.

The left foot is used as a guide or pointer.

Use a bent arm position with the ball held behind your right ear.

The throw should be overhand and quick.

Your body should go in the direction of the throw.

When fielding ground balls in front of home plate, use two hands, with the glove acting as a scoop.

TAKING OFF THE MASK TO CATCH

When you have a lot of time to catch a pop fly, throw your mask away from where you are going.

If you don't have much time, knock the mask off with your thumb and run toward the ball.

The sun, the wind, and how close you are to the dugout or stands, are things to think about when you take your mask off and throw it during a play.

JUDGING POP FLIES

Stand here for a pop fly over or in front of home plate, which is fair territory.

Pop flies hit directly over home plate or just in front of it will curve away from you. Play this ball just off your head.

Stand here for a pop fly behind home plate, which is foul territory.

Pop flies hit behind home plate will curve back to you. Play this ball away from your body.

TAGGING AT THE PLATE

Tag the runner by holding the ball with your ungloved hand within the glove.

THE WAY TO STAND

Keep your toes pointed slightly out.

Bend your knees slightly.

Lean your body forward.

Don't have your weight on your heels.

Don't spread your feet far apart.

Don't keep your knees straight.

Don't point your toes in.

Watch the hitter's bat.

Crossover step when going to the right or left side

FIELDING THE BALL

Control the ball, don't let it control you.

A ball with a short hop or a big hop is the easiest to control.

Move toward the ball. When in doubt—charge!

Field the ball in front of your body.

Keep your eyes on the ball and follow it to the glove.

Keep your legs apart, knees bent, backside low, arms and hands in front of your body.

Catching the ball with two hands is better than one because your throwing hand is already on the ball.

Playing the hop

THROWING THE BALL

Practice getting into a good throwing position.

Look where you are throwing.

Follow through.

Use a short, arm-snap throw. Infielders don't have much time.

Make a "soft throw"—backspin on the ball.

INFIELDERS MUST KNOW

The number of outs

Which way the wind is blowing

Where the batter hits the ball most of the time

How fast the batter runs

USE YOUR VOICE ON POP FLIES

It is important to yell!

Help your teammate by shouting, "I've got it!" Your teammate should answer, "Take it."

TAGGING THE RUNNERS

**The proper tagging position
Runner is sliding into the glove.**

As infielder you must remember that the baserunner tags himself out.

Place your feet on both sides of the base.

Catch the ball with both hands, but put the gloved hand down and in front of the base, so that the runner "tags himself out."

Do not reach out and tag the runner.

THE FIRST BASEMAN

As first baseman, you should be able to stretch for throws, pick up balls in the ground, and move on bad throws.

Waiting for the infielder's throw

Moving to both sides

Moving to the right

Moving to the left

The Way to Stand

Watch the fat end of the bat.

Your knees are bent.

Your weight is on the front part of your feet.

Your hands are low and ready.

Where to Stand with a Runner on First Base

After the pitcher throws toward home plate, move into fair ground a bit more.

THE SECOND BASEMAN

The Double Play

The second baseman and the shortstop should move in a step or two toward the batter.

Get about one to three steps closer to second base, depending on who is at bat.

(When you are a young, new player, it is best to run to second base as quickly as possible, and with a foot on either side of the base, throw to first base.)

As you get more experience, here are other ways to make the double play:

Dragging your left foot over second base
Stepping on the bag with your left foot
Stepping on the bag with your right foot
Shifting toward left field and dragging the left foot

Double Play # 1

Drags left foot, steps on right foot, and throws to first base

When the shortstop gives the ball to the second baseman, he throws the ball at his face. Use underhand if close, but a snap overhand throw if you are more than twelve feet away.

Dragging left foot over the base

Start of throw to first base

Turning and throwing the ball

Double Play # 2

Stepping on the base with your left foot

Push off base with your left foot, placing your weight on the right foot and throw to first base.

Double Play # 3

Throw off your right foot as you step toward first base.

The way to stand while catching the ball

Double Play # 4

When the ball is thrown to your right

The shift—your weight is on the right foot.

The pivot, or turn and throw—your weight is on the left foot.

THE SHORTSTOP

The best ways to make the double plays are:

Dragging your right foot on the outer edge of second base

Stepping on second base with your left foot

Making the double play by yourself

(For new players, it might be best to start with number one and practice the other two when you have more experience.)

Double play # 1

Drag right toes on outer edge of second base.

Take a short hop, place your weight on your right foot, and throw to first base.

Double Play # 2

Step on the base with your left foot,
shift your weight to your right foot,
and throw to first base.

The inside pivot or turn and throw to
first base

Double Play # 3

When you field the ball close to second base, you can make the double play yourself.

Start your throw before you touch second base.

Tag the base with your left foot, before you throw to first base.

The shortstop making the double play alone

THE THIRD BASEMAN

As third baseman, you should have a strong arm and an accurate throw.

You must get in front of hard-hit balls, and you must be quick.

The third baseman has to know when hitters will try to bunt. Watch the batter's hand. When the top hand moves up the bat, it may be a bunt.

Slow batted balls are tough plays. These plays are between the pitcher's box and the foul line. The best way to make this play is with your ungloved hand. It's a one-hand pickup and throw.

A big play is the throw to second base on the double play. The throw should be at face level even if you take a little longer. When your team is ahead in a close game, and when you are near the end of the game, the third baseman guards the line.

A good outfielder gets a good start on all balls hit to the outfield.

THE WAY TO STAND

The toes are pointed slightly out. This lets you move quickly in any direction.

The knees are bent, with your weight evenly spread on both feet.

The hands are placed on the knees or alongside your body.

Watch the fat part of the bat.

THE CROSSOVER STEP

The crossover step should be used whenever you go to your left or right.

When a fly ball is in the sun, you should shade the sun with your glove. Look over or under the glove until you catch the ball.

Shading the sun   **Catching the ball**

Whenever you can, catch the ball with both hands. Just as the ball is caught, there is a slight give or pulling of the hands and wrist toward your body.

Run on your toes when you are going after fly balls. Heel running jars your body and makes it hard to see to catch the ball.

PLAYING THE WALL

Run to the fence first, then alongside it.

It may be that you are playing in parks that don't have fences. When you do, this is how to play the fly ball near the fence. Baseball people call it "playing the wall."

When you have to throw quickly, you should catch the ball on your throwing side and have your body moving forward when you throw.

Catching the ball in throwing position   **The correct throw**

USE YOUR VOICE

Calling plays in the outfield is important. Outfielders should help each other by calling, "Lots of room. You have it!"

When fly balls are hit between two outfielders, the outfielder in the better position to catch the ball yells, "I've got it!" The other outfielder answers, "Take it!"

The center fielder is the "captain" of the outfield. When he yells, "I've got it!" then either the right or left fielder says, "Take it!"

HELMETS

Wear your helmet during batting practice.

The regular helmet

The earflap helmet

The earflap helmet is the best kind. Try to wear one. It protects the head, the ears, and the sides of the face.

You should also use the helmet when running the bases. Play safety first.

REMEMBER

Keep bats and balls off the field of play.

Don't stand behind batters while they are swinging.

Don't throw the bat after you make a hit.

Make sure all equipment and your uniform fit well.

Your sweatshirt, inner stockings, and other clothing and equipment should be kept clean.

Cuts can become infected and cause a lot of trouble.

Don't warm up close to another player when you are throwing. A wild pitch which hits someone in the face happens mostly when players are too close together.

Stay alert, be heads-up, and concentrate on every play!

Have a good year.

SLANG TERMS USED IN BASEBALL

Baltimore Chop   A ball hit across its top, which makes it bounce high up in the air

Banjo Hit   A short fly ball just over the infield

Bean Ball   A pitch thrown at a hitter's head

Bench Warmer   A player who seldom plays in a game

Bleeder   A "lucky hit," or a scratch hit

Blooper   Same as a "banjo hit"

Boot   An error, or a missed ground ball

Bullpen   The area where starters and relief pitchers warm up

Bushes   The minor leagues, or the "sticks"

Change Up   A slow pitch, also known as "let up"

Choke Grip   Gripping the bat a few inches up from the end of the handle

Clean Up   The #4 batter position in the lineup

Clutch Hitter   A hitter who bats well when it counts

Cousin   A batter who hits well off a certain pitcher

Cripple   Three balls and one strike, and two balls and no strikes, because they are good pitches to hit

Cycle   A single, double, triple and homerun hit by one player in one game

Dish   Home plate

Duster   A pitch so close to a hitter's head that it makes him hit the dirt

Foot in Bucket   Pulling away from home plate

Full Count   Three balls and two strikes on the batter

Goat   Player whose mistake lost the game

Gopher Ball   Pitch hit for a homerun

Grand Slam   A bases-loaded homerun

Hill   The pitcher's box, the rubber

Hook   A curve ball

Hot Corner   Third base

Jockey   A player who worries or "gets on" the opposition

Keystone   Second base

Leatherman   A good fielder, one with good hands

Leg Hitter   A runner who beats out many hits because of good running speed. He has "good wheels."

On Deck   A player in the "on deck" circle, waiting to hit

Pass   A walk, a stroll, a base on balls

Pinch Hitter   A substitute batter

Portsider   A south paw, a lefthanded pitcher

Pulling a Rock   Making a dumb play

Relief pitcher   A pitcher who comes in during a game to substitute for the starting pitcher

Rookie   A first year player

Sack   A base, bag, cushion

Shutout   No runs scored, a blank job

Texas Leaguer   Short fly ball between infield and outfield for a hit

Woodman   A good batter